Happy 16th Birthday

Made in the USA
Monee, IL
13 June 2022

97938219R00069